Images of
Wigan

Wigan Evening Post

Images of Wigan

Breedon Books
Publishing Company
Derby

First published in Great Britain by
The Breedon Books Publishing Company Limited
44 Friar Gate, Derby, DE1 1DA.
1995

ISBN 1 85983 008 0

Printed and bound by Butler & Tanner, Frome, Somerset.
Cover printed by Premier Print, Nottingham.

Contents

Introduction

METROPOLITAN Wigan is a unique area. Since the 1974 local government reorganisation the borough has comprised of 14 towns and several smaller villages – yet each locality has retained its own distinct identity and its own treasured traditions.

There were those who thought that such an amorphous arrangement of local authorities would not work, but time has reinforced this unity.

As long ago as 1246 the Wigan area was regarded as a place of such trading importance as to justify the town receiving Royal recognition as a borough from the reigning monarch, Henry III.

Before the Romans came to Britain, Wigan district was mainly forest and marshland occupied by a Celtic tribe known as the Brigantes. They were conquered by the Romans who built a fort at Wigan. Roman remains have been unearthed in Millgate and at other places in the town over the years.

After the Romans withdrew, the Anglo-Saxon settlers moved into the area followed, around AD 900, by the Vikings and then the Norman barons.

Medieval remains can still be found in Wigan – Mab's Cross in Standishgate is one of them. By the thirteenth century, Wigan was a prosperous walled town with its four main streets – Wallgate, Standishgate, Millgate and Hallgate – all converging on Market Place.

Coal was being dug up in the Wigan area as far back as the fourteenth century. The first coal-pit was dug in Millgate in 1619 and soon pits were being sunk in many local areas.

In the early years of the seventeenth century, conflict occurred between Parliament and the Stuart monarchy which raged for over a century. Wigan remained loyal to Royalty throughout the Civil War, but in 1643 Cromwell's army captured Wigan. The final Lancashire battle of the Civil War was fought in 1651 at Wigan Lane on the banks of the River Douglas. A monument there marks the spot where Royalist Sir Thomas Tyldesley was killed in battle.

By the beginning of the Victorian age Britain was becoming the workshop of the world with its growing new industries – and all of these depended on coal. It was around this time that Wigan began developing three great industries – mining, cotton and engineering.

The town's population grew rapidly as rural folk foresook their cottage industries to seek work in the new mills, foundries and coal-mines.

Wigan was one of the richest coalfields in the country and it brought prosperity for some and misery for others. It was not until an Act of 1847 that the cruel exploitation of children working underground was forbidden. From then on the pit brow lasses remained above ground riddling and shovelling the coal into waggons and barges.

As Wigan's population increased, hundreds of small back-to-back houses were built, resulting in wretched living accommodation. The number of public houses also grew. By 1880 there was almost one pub on every street corner which opened from early morning until late at night. Later Wigan developed a strong sporting tradition which it has maintained until this day, mainly in rugby and soccer. Wigan RL club have now won just about every trophy there is to win and is at the forefront of a move towards a European 'super league'.

The second largest town in the metropolitan borough is Leigh, which was formed as a parish in the twelfth century. It, too, developed into an important coal-mining and textile area in the nineteenth century and was noted also for its silk weaving.

Few places in Britain have undergone such a vast face lift as Metropolitan Wigan which has changed out of all recognition with many of its old buildings and traditional industries having been swept away. The fortunes of the borough now revolve around new and cleaner industries.

The numerous old photographs shown in this book provide an interesting illustrated historical record of the Wigan area's past and are a tribute to the courage and comradeship of its people.

Foreword

By Councillor Bernard Holt, Mayor of Wigan Metropolitan Borough.

Wigan is a thoroughly modern place with plenty to be proud of in today's world, but that is precisely because the achievements of today are built on the values and principles of the people who built Wigan's proud past.

I am delighted to welcome this new book, which will remind everyone of the hard work involved in Wigan's rich history. The town's prosperity was built on coal, cotton and the railways. For the people who dug the coal, spun the cotton and laid the tracks, life was often cruel, and yet Wigan has always retained its sense of humour.

These wonderfully nostalgic pictures are a celebration of the solid worth of Wiganers of yesteryear, and will be a most appropriate forerunner for our 750th Market Charter anniversary in 1996.

Shadows of the Past

The worst of the working-class houses built at the time of the Industrial Revolution occurred before development controls were introduced. Many houses had only one outside wall and pail as communal closets. Rylance Row (seen here) off Standishgate, is just one example in 1900. Note the bulging walls.

This bleak scene in Wood's Yard, off Duke Street, Wigan Lane, depicts life in the town around 1902 before local planning was improved.

This was known as part of the Irish quarter in Wigan. Scholes was in a poorer quarter of the town which attracted many of the immigrants during the Irish famine years.

This row of cottages in Douglas Terrace was demolished after World War Two. Most of the houses had no running water and no sewerage system. Communal lavatories for the whole of the street were situated at the bottom of the terrace with only one tap for all the residents. In 1246, when Wigan officially became a borough, it was then an elegant thoroughfare.

The pride of the 1720s. This rare old photograph shows Wigan Town Hall which was built in 1720 and demolished in 1882. It stood in the Market Hall in front of the Transport Offices. In its later years the Town Hall ground floor was turned into butchers' booths and became known as the Shambles. King Street Town Hall was built in 1868.

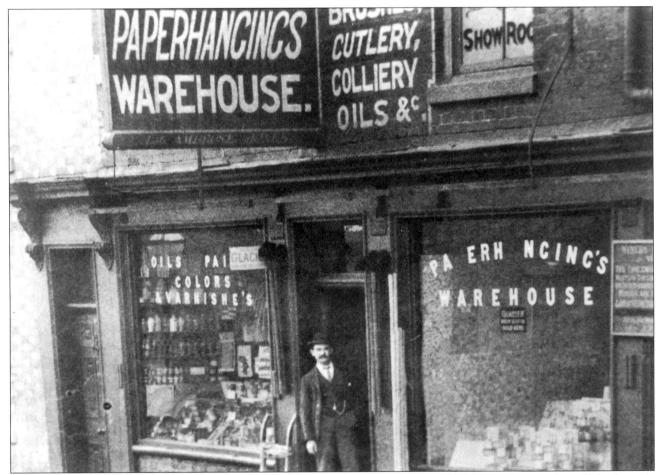

No mistaking what goods he sold. Len Fletcher's Edwardian warehouse at 35 Millgate was demolished some years ago. Next door to it was the Miners Federation local branch.

Millgate, once one of the busiest streets in the town centre, enjoys life in the slower lane compared with this scene 25 years ago.

Millgate, Wigan, around 1940.

A rare view of Wallgate in the early twentieth century when the bank on the left was being built.

Wallgate Station is still there – but changed and the trams have long since vanished.

Wallgate, Wigan, as it was in 1950.

Standishgate in 1857. The entrance to 'Little London' which has since been widened.

The lower part of Standishgate around 1890, before Mesnes Street was made. On the right is the original store of Pendlebury & Co with its pillared entrance.

Grayson's Yard in 1901. Only a few yards from comparatively stylish Standishgate, it was an area of sub-standard housing for many years. Many families had to eat and sleep in one room.

Standishgate around 1910 from the brow of the hill. The hoardings to the left became the site of St Mary's and St John's combined schools. On the right Mab's Cross Hotel with the historic landmark across the road.

Standishgate at the turn of the century. The gaslamp has now disappeared and so have the cobblestones.

Standishgate in 1939 with the Three Crowns on the left. Notice the limited rear view windows in the cars at that time and also the boot doors which opened downwards.

The old traffic lights at the bottom of Standishgate in 1940.

This is a glimpse of Wigan in the 'Swinging Sixties'. The famous old skyline was snapped in 1968 at the top of Standishgate. Westminster Bank (left) later changed to NatWest and F.W.Woolworth became John Menzies.

Remember the Rendezvous? It stood on Standishgate and when this photograph was taken around 1945 it is thought the folks outside were in celebratory mood for the end of the war.

The first decade of this century was a harsh one in the Wigan area and pawnbrokers like this one did a busy trade. These premises were in Market Street, Wigan.

Market Street, Wigan, in 1890. The Crofters Arms is on the left.

Sawbridge's butchers in Market Street, Wigan, clearly had no fears about hygiene regulations in 1895. The shop supplied meat at that time to Lord Crawford, who then owned Haigh Hall estate.

The old Market Hall Wigan as it was around 1918 – and now replaced by the modern Galleries.

Market Square, Wigan, in 1935 did a booming trade selling all kinds of produce – most of it from the farmers' carts. They were said to have the cheapest produce in Lancashire.

A high vantage point view of Market Place, Wigan's main shopping area, as it looked in 1913. Electric trams in the town centre ceased running in 1931 and one-way traffic was introduced in the 1960s.

Food trolleys, self-service and computer check-outs were still unheard of when this photograph was taken at Peterkin's, grocers, on the corner of Hallgate and Market Street, Wigan in 1950. A smile and cheery welcome was always assured from the staff. Peterkin's was later taken over by Fine Fare in 1956 and these premises later sold sportswear.

Queen's Hall Methodist Mission and neighbouring shops in Market Street as they appeared in 1939.

Market Place, Wigan, in the 'Roaring Twenties'. The trams have now given way to the buses and the gaslamp in the foreground has gone, along with the signposts.

Old curiosity shops like this one have long disappeared from Wigan town centre. The Wigan Mourning Warehouse Co sold mantles and costumes from Makinson Arcade. Hanging from the shop front is the sign showing the figure of woman wearing a black mourning coat, skirt and hat. Deep mourning often used to last up to a year in many families.

Michael Marks, one of the founders of Marks & Spencer lived in St George Street, Wigan, for a time. He opened a Penny Bazaar in the Market Hall in 1891 and for some years the town was the centre of his operations. This picture was taken in 1925 outside Marks & Spencer's store which was then in Makinson Arcade.

The staff of Marks & Spencer's store in Makinson Arcade in 1925, showing off a window full of buckets.

Makinsons Arcade, Wigan, shows its patriotism in 1945. The arcade was first opened in 1913.

The Minorca Hotel, Wallgate, as it looked around 1900. Reference to an inn on the site goes back to 1791 in a deed between William Roper and the Corporation 'to make a street between Wallgate, Chapel Lane and Millgate'.

Mab's Cross in 1950 inside the grounds of the then Girls' High School. Lady Mable, legend says, had to walk barefoot in 1315 once a week for a year from her home at Haigh to the cross at Standishgate. This penance was imposed by her husband Sir William de Bradshaigh for wrongly presuming his death in battle.

This is how Wallgate looked in 1953.

Conroy Bros, wholesale fruit merchants, had traded in Wigan since 1916. Behind is the Park Hotel once noted for good ale. Both premises vanished to make way for the Galleries Market Hall.

The Royal Albert Edward Infirmary took its name from the Prince of Wales who opened it in 1873. The hospital at first mainly treated accident victims because of its location among the mines and mills of Wigan. The infirmary frontage has changed since this 1920s view.

The Upper Johnson Children's Ward in Wigan's Royal Albert Edward Infirmary in 1910. The sparse furnishing and basic lighting is a far cry from the pleasant atmosphere of today's children's wards.

A sedate scene with tramcar and a horse-drawn carriage passing Plantation Gates around 1910.

The Rushton Bros once had almost 60 shops in the Wigan area. This is grocery branch No 56 in 1925, which was in Mesnes Road. The business was founded by George and Oates Rushton who came to Wigan from Yorkshire in 1870 to set up shop in the Market Place. The family business was sold in 1952.

George Orwell slept here! The author of *The Road to Wigan Pier* (1937) lodged above this corner shop while researching for his famous book. It was a tripe shop in those days.

Polly Sherrington's small grocery shop (centre) sold nearly everything on Scholes. The shop was demolished in the 1960s.

A quiet corner in Brock Mill Lane in 1960 which time doesn't seem to change. The road leads to the Douglas Valley past the former mill that was once the home of the *Evening Post and Chronicle*, now long gone.

Wigan Road, Ashton-in-Makerfield, around 1945.

A landmark which fell to the bulldozer. Rainford House was built in Winstanley in 1665 but sadly it was demolished in 1967 to make way for housing development.

Wrightington Hall as it looked in the early 1920s.

Gerard Street, Ashton-in-Makerfield, enjoyed traffic-free days when this was taken in 1939. The name Gerard has historic links with the area.

Gerard Street, Ashton-in-Makerfield, as it looked around 1939. On the forefront right is the Gerard Arms.

Church Street Gardens, Leigh, in 1908.

Kerfoot's grocery shop in Market Street, Leigh, in 1893, where the Town Hall now stands.

Whittles chemists in Market Street, Leigh, was demolished in 1899 for road widening. It was noted for selling odd items such as purging drink for cows and perfumed handkerchiefs.

Meadow Dairy Co's shop in Bradshawgate, Leigh, in 1937 was a far cry from today's supermarket trading. It stood directly opposite the F.W.Woolworth store.

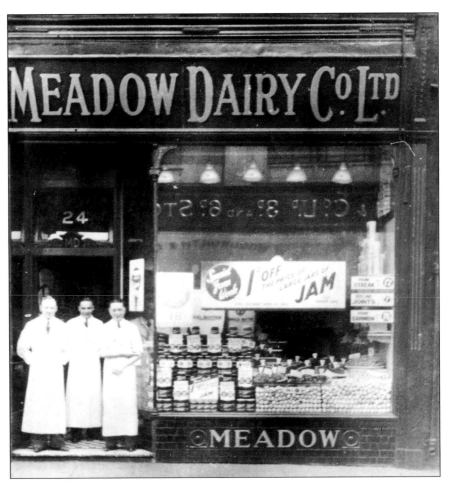

Pennington Hall, Leigh, was for centuries one of the most important houses in the area. It was occupied by the Atherton family, lords of the manor and later owned by the Lilfords. Pennington Hall was later demolished and the site became a public parkland.

Ward Bros on the corner of Stanley Street and Elliott Street in Tyldesley proudly welcomed the visit of King George V and Queen Mary to the area in 1913.

Bottling Wood, Whelley, will evoke memories for some people. It was a community where everybody, it is said, knew everybody and loved to help each other. In the background is Alexander Colliery. Bottling is a derivative of Butler, the family who once owned the wood.

A view of Whelley in 1900 looking towards Scholes. The cottages have been replaced with modern dwellings. Two hostelries in this area were the George and Dragon and the Miners' Tent.

Manor House, a historic building that used to stand in Scholes, towards Whelley.

Smile for the birdie – even the local bobby wanted to be on this photograph taken in the Scholes area in 1900. At this time Scholes was a much depressed area.

The old gamekeeper's lodge in the grounds of Haigh Hall Country Park.

The Pony Dick Inn (left) in Billinge Road, had several different names in the early nineteenth century and got its name from the favourite white pony of Squire Meysick Bankers. The pony died aged 36 in 1841 and was buried near Winstanley Hall. His gravestone is still there.

Hindley House, Wigan, built in the late eighteenth century, was the home of several notable families including Ackers Colliery owners and George Formby's family.

No traffic light terrors when this picture was taken – just turnpike ones! This turnpike was across Ladies Lane, Hindley. The tolls were collected by the keeper whose house was alongside and the money went towards maintaining the road.

Hogston's, 'The people's tea shop', was the proud claim of this corner shop No.33 Market Street, Atherton, around 1900.

Shopkeepers stand proudly outside their premises in Wigan Lane and youngsters pause in order to be on this picture in 1921.

Winstanley's ice cream in Orrell Road were proud to announce in the 1920s that their product was made by electricity.

Corner shops have virtually all gone. This one, in the late 1920s, was John Coleclough's, Warrington Road, Goose Green.

The old Marylebone Post Office, Wigan Lane, and the adjacent cottages. Sadly they are no longer there.

Sub-Post Offices are becoming fewer and fewer. At one time they were part of close-knit communities. This one, shown in 1925, was in Spring View and was owned by Miss Jane Nevin (centre). Next to her is her brother and his wife. Post Offices, it will be recalled, used to sell lots of other items as well.

School Lane, Up Holland, near Wigan. The village once ranked as important as many of the larger market towns of its day. The Holland family dated back to Richard III.

Prison, court house, cloggers' shop, dwelling house – that was the chequered career of this famous old building on School Lane, Up Holland. It was built in 1683 and in 1927 the local council gave permission for its conversion to a private dwelling, so long as it retained its old character.

Wigan at Work

The Owd Clog Shop at Up Holland. At 86 years of age, master clogger Richard Baxter was still hammering away at his bench.

Clarington Forge in Wigan is part of the town's history. It dates back to 1789 when it was first established by William Park at the site in Darlington Street East. These are workers at the forge with a selection of tools made at the factory between Wigan and Ince. In 1929 a subsidiary of William Park Ltd was set up at the forge, producing industrial and agricultural hand tools.

Hammer heads, steel nails, nuts, screws and almost anything metal could be made by Wigan's forgemaster William Park & Co. Formed as a limited company in 1938 it was successor to a business which had been in existence for more than 150 years to make colliery winding gear. This is one of the firm's 2,000-ton forging presses.

One of Wigan's former best-known engineering firms was Walker Brothers, at Pagefield Ironworks which grew from small beginnings in 1886 off Queen Street, then to Springfield in 1873. Production continued there for over a century under the ownership of Walmsley's of Bury, until the foundry closed and a new one was built in Bolton.

Another well-known forge mill, that of Park Webb Limited, at their Ince Forge. This huge 4-ton hammer was photographed in use in 1970 and finished its working life there in 1979.

The iron industry played a big part in former days. The firm of William Park, at School Common, began in 1787. It later became known as Park Webb Limited. Their products ranged from nails to steam engines. This is the company's machine shop in World War One.

Haigh Foundry closed down over 110 years ago, but recollections of it are still related among older folk.
This picture depicts the site of the one-time heart of Haigh.

The *SS Thomas* leaving Wigan Pier in bygone days with passengers. Barges were used for passenger
transport from the Leeds-Liverpool Canal's first opening in 1777.

A gloomy, drab scene at Wigan Pier in 1958, but it seems it provided this artist with inspiration.

A barge on a section of the Bridgewater Canal at Leigh as it looked in 1985. This canal was built around 1895 to link Wigan indirectly with the Manchester Ship Canal.

Wigan Pier, as seen here in 1968, was known as a run-down wreck.

Earning their crust! Young bakery men at Bamford's Mountain Bakery, Wright Street, Whelley, in 1905.

Many elderly people in the Wigan area will have strong memories of their days in the mills. This picture was taken in Thomas Taylor's giant weaving shed.

Other workers at Thomas Taylor's mill sat for hours hand-stitching clothing beside wooden desks – not a glamorous occupation but they were glad of a chance to earn a little money.

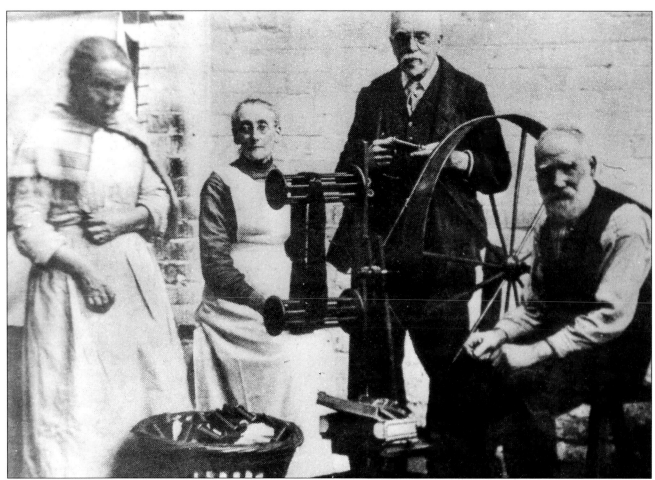

Employees of George Hilton's hand-woven silk mill in Leigh which closed its doors in 1926 after falling victim to foreign competition.

An old Leigh silk spinner at her wheel.

The spinning room in one of Wigan's former numerous cotton mills.

This semi-wasteland in front of the large building was transformed into what is now beautiful Mesnes Park in Wigan. The land belonged to the Rector of Wigan and it was eventually given to the town and developed into scenic parkland. The factory in the background was the old Rylands Cotton Mill which indicates what a booming industry cotton once was in Wigan. After closure the mill was taken over by a mail-order firm.

Bobbin winding at Trencherfield Mill played an important role in the cotton spinning industry.

As late as 1950 young mill workers of 14 had to work long hours compared with those of today's work-force. They started at 7.45am and worked until 5.30pm with half an hour for midday lunch. This 14-year-old spinning doffer can still smile despite the heavy bobbins she has to carry.

Each year before World War Two, North-West cotton mill towns elected a mill worker as 'Cotton Queen'. The North-West finalist was elected at the Tower Ballroom, Blackpool. Here is the Wigan Cotton Queen 1939, with Ince St John Ambulance at the New Year's Eve dance. Guest of honour was Mr William McCracken, manager of the Empress Cotton mill.

Wigan was once the centre of the Lancashire cotton industry. Sadly, this was the last of the town's weaving mills. The factory gates of Dorma-Eckersleys, in Swan Meadows Mill, 14 Meadows Lane, closed in 1988 and was later converted to industrial units.

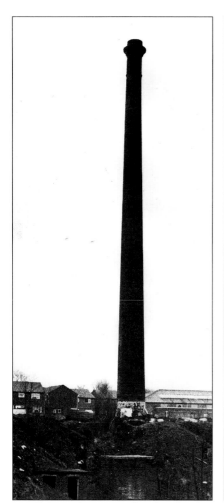

All it took was 10lb of gelignite and the touch of a button to cause the 200ft famous 100-year-old Wigan landmark at May Mill, Pemberton, to disappear from the skyline in 1985. Going! Going! Gone!

A smiling mop and bucket brigade take time off to pose for the camera in the 'Hungry Thirties'. These Mrs Mops were all cleaners at the Court Cinema in King Street, Wigan.

Coop's clothing factory in Dorning Street used to employ many operatives. It was founded by a local tailor, Timothy Coop, who in 1872 hit on the idea of training girls to use sewing machines for mass production. This rare photograph was taken in 1892, from Wigan Parish Church gardens showing King Street West and the County Court (right) in Crawford Street. Coop's factory received planning permission in 1994 for use as flats and other developments.

Clothing factory founder Timothy Coop.

Heinz products have become known
all over the world since Henry J.Heinz
started out in a small way in 1844.
The company first moved to Kitt
Green, Wigan, in 1949 from the south
of England. This picture shows the
Wigan factory soon after it first
opened.

The man who founded the famous 57 Varieties
– Henry J.Heinz. When he was only 16 he
began selling vegetables he had grown at his
home in Pennsylvania, USA. Later he began
bottling them for sale. When he was 42 he
came to London and began selling his products
to Fortnum & Mason and from then on his
business grew.

One of the earlier Heinz family members at the firm's first food trade exhibition in 1909.

The 'Hello Girls' at Wigan Telephone Exchange in the 1920s give a quick sideways glance at the camera under the watchful eye of their supervisors. Micro chips and computer controls were still a long way off.

These women look happy at their work in the canning department at De Haan (Foods) Ltd in 1961.

This is the pickling department of De Haan (Foods) Ltd.

The mighty Westwood Power Station, Wigan, as it looked during construction in 1950.

These mighty water cooling towers just completed in 1950 soared 314ft into the air and could be seen all over Wigan.

A big crowd gathered in 1989 to bid farewell to the two massive cooling towers at Westwood Power Station. The twin cooling towers and the twin chimneys alongside had dominated the Wigan skyline for many years.

Four months after the demolition of the cooling towers the two-giant Westwood chimneys were also demolished. The Mayor of Angers, Wigan's French twin town, pressed the detonating plunger which brought the first chimney down. The other was blasted by a local man who won the privilege in a charity draw.

Black Diamonds

Pit brow lasses was the term given to female colliery workers. After they were banned from working underground by Parliament they continued to work at the pit surface until as late as the 1950s. The girls pictured here are at Moss Hall Colliery in 1908.

The pin-up girls of the past! The pit brow lasses who sorted and washed the coal at the pit head were a hard-working set.

Another glimpse of the pit brow lasses of yesteryear. This time it is the girls of Shevington Basket Pit who pose for the camera.

This picture shows the tough conditions that the pit brow lasses had to endure for a meagre wage. Working with bare hands in a cold, draughty shed for long hours was a gruelling task.

Pit brow lasses at the Maypole Pit in the 1920s. Seems like all the policemen in Wigan wanted to be on the photograph too – or was it just police protection?

These pit brow lasses looked spruce and clean in the 1930s so that they could wave to King George V when he was passing J & R Stone's Colliery, Liverpool Road, Ashton, on his way to open the nearby new East Lancashire Road.

Women check weighers at Douglas Bank Colliery. Their job was to check the weight of coal produced by the men on each shift. The colliery was in Woodhouse Lane, Wigan.

Pit brow lasses at Strangeways Colliery in 1910. It was owned by Crompton and Shawcross. The lasses pose with their wickerwork lunch baskets before clocking on.

These girls at Mains Colliery, Bamfurlong, in the 1930s are seen taking a break from stacking pit props which the miners used for tunnel roof supports.

Pit brow lasses in 1936 at Garswood Hall Colliery. Their job was phased out in the 1950s with the introduction of automatic washers.

Little Polly Harrison and her pit brow colleagues were all spruced up for this retirement presentation around 1944 at Mains Colliery, Wigan. Her presentation gift for a lifetime's hard work at the pit was contained in the parcel she has just received – it was a cardigan!

All clean and trim before starting their work at Maypole Colliery, Abram, these pit brow lasses were among the last to be photographed in 1949 before the pit eventually closed in 1958.

Horse-drawn coal carts like C.H.Pedder's used to be a common sight in Wigan area streets. Many merchants used to go around the streets shouting out the price of their coal.

This bleak photograph of Wigan Pier appeared in the one-time popular weekly national magazine *Picture Post* in 1939. The periodical went on to say that Wigan was aiming to be the 'best planned borough in the county'.

Wigan Coal and Iron Works at Kirkless, is an industry that has long vanished. The huge structure used to be a familiar sight in the New Springs area of Wigan and was known locally as Top Place. Smoking chimneys spelt work and wages for sweating miners and foundry workers.

Wigan Pier's cabin was a famous landmark for years in the town. It stood on the side of the old railway where it crossed Warrington Road at Goose Green. Actually there were several piers in Wigan which were used to load coal into the moored barges. Sadly, Wigan Pier and the rail line closed in 1929.

A knocker-up of long ago. Some knocker-ups were paid by the colliery to awaken their employees while some had rounds of their own which included mill workers' homes. Alarm clocks were too costly for many people.

The people of Wigan area have always been able to accept jokes at the expense of themselves. This is one of the postcards dated around 1905 that poked fun at the numerous dingy slag heaps in the area. It was captioned 'The Alps, Higher Ince'.

Pemberton Colliery, seen here in 1931, was once the biggest in the country. It closed in 1946. During the 1926 General Strike, miners began to dig their own coal from shallow pits and it was discovered there was surface coal in nearby Blundell Wood.

The old King, Queen and Prince pits at Pemberton Colliery.

Wigan coalfield was noted for its special type of coal known as 'cannel' which was of high quality and shiny. It was once popular for carving into ornaments. This 11-ton block of cannel was obtained from Junction Colliery, Abram, in 1880.

This photograph was seen throughout Britain in 1939 in the famous national magazine *Picture Post*. It shows a sorry line of Wigan unemployed outside a Labour Exchange waiting to 'sign on'. The *Post* said that 17 of the 40 coal-pits in the area were closed.

In a bid to get coal from the ground more quickly during World War Two, open-cast mining was started in the Wigan coalfield area.

A brooding colliery slag heap contrasts sharply with a pastoral scene near Wigan in 1950. Thankfully the ugly heaps are now gone.

Maypole Colliery, Abram, as it looked in 1959.

Summersales Colliery had a unique claim to fame. Its short life lasted from 1944 to 1966 and it had one of the shallowest shafts in Lancashire – only 54ft deep.

NCB trainees in the 1950s at the Low Hall Mining Training Centre, Platt Bridge.

British Coal claimed to be the world leaders in land restoration. This was the scene of Amberswood opencast site, Hindley, before 1987.

And this was the more pleasant scene of Amberswood afterwards.

Tragedy

One of the worst coal-mine disasters in the Wigan area occurred at Wood Pit, Haydock, in 1878, when more than 200 men and boys lost their lives. It was caused by a fire-damp explosion which robbed the mine of air. This is how the *Illustrated London News* reproduced a scene of the identification of the dead in the mortuary. In the 1910 Pretoria Pit, Wigan, explosion 334 men and boys were killed.

One of the blackest days in Wigan's coal-mining history was on 18 August 1908 at the Maypole Colliery, Park Lane, Abram. An explosion 3,000ft underground killed 76 men. The day shift, luckily, had just left otherwise hundreds more would have perished. Even buildings on the surface were damaged as this old photograph shows.

Calm before the firestorm! This was the quiet, leisurely scene at Maypole Colliery, Abram, on 18 August 1908, only minutes before the terrible fatal explosion occurred. Fortunately, these colliers had not reached the pit for their shift when the blast, which killed 76, occurred.

This melancholy scene shows the funeral of one of the Maypole Colliery victims of the 1908 disaster. Explosions could be heard beneath the ground around Abram for weeks after the first violent blast in August that year.

One of the many graphic postcard mementoes of the Maypole Colliery disaster of 1908, sold to raise funds for relief of victims' families.

The driver of this engine was killed along with a woman passenger when his train left the line at Hindley in July 1900. The train was carrying holidaymakers from Blackpool to Dewsbury.

Sombre dignity marked the horse-drawn funeral cortèges of yesteryear. The top-hatted drivers and the magnificently groomed horses were employed by funeral directors Middleton & Wood. This picture was taken around 1920 in King Street, Wigan.

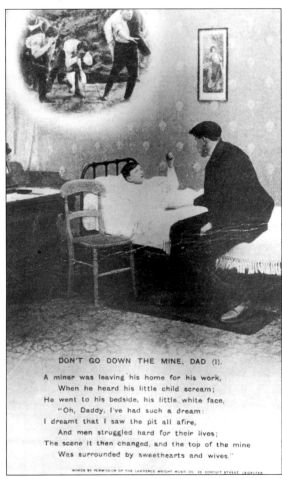

Don't Go Down the Mine, Dad was one of the heart-rending ballads of the Victorian and Edwardian era. This one told how a young son's dream premonition of a mining disaster saved his father's life.

Grieving neighbours in Gerard Street, Ashton-in-Makerfield, line the funeral cortège route of one of the victims of the pit explosion of 1932 which claimed the lives of 27 men. Many more were badly injured and nearly every family knew someone in the closely-knit community who had been killed or injured in the Edge Green Colliery tragedy.

This Wigan family's happiness turned to tragic sadness a year after this picture was taken on a Blackpool outing in 1910. It shows Jim Green, a miner at Bamfurlong Colliery, with his wife Eliza and their three children. Jim received the Carnegie Hero's award when, along with others, he carried out the dramatic rescue of 11 comrades in the flooded colliery. Jim contracted pneumonia as a result and died shortly before he was due to receive his medal.

Blundell Colliery rescue team in 1914. After the Maypole Colliery disaster of 1908, blasting in a pit was
forbidden until it had been cleared of miners except those who were to do the blasting.

This stained-
glass window
in St Thomas'
Church,
Golborne,
bears the
names of five
of the ten men
killed in the
Golborne pit
disaster on 18
March 1979. A
methane gas
explosion
ripped through
the pit which
was closed
about ten years
later because it
was said to be
unprofitable.

Turmoil and War

The chief constable of Wigan, William Simms, who with his small force, was pelted with stones while trying to disperse colliers and cotton workers in the 1853 strike. The violence developed after strike-breakers were brought into the town from Wales.

Pemberton Colliery's four-month lock-out led to the setting up of this Pony Dick Soup Kitchen Committee at the end of last century. Other soup kitchens were set up in pubs like the Blundells Arms, the Railway Hotel and the Castle Inn, to relieve hardship.

The chief constable's soup kitchen in 1893 for miners' children.

Scenes like this, showing hundreds of miners scratching for coal, were all too common during the miners'
lock-out of 1893. The bitter dispute began when their pay was slashed by 25 per cent. The miners refused to
accept and were locked out for four weary months.

Hungry children waiting for the Bowling Green Hotel, Wigan, soup kitchen to open during the 1893 miners'
lock-out.

Some of the helpers at the Bowling Green Hotel soup kitchen during the gruelling 1893 dispute.

The Revd William Wickham, Vicar of Wigan, helps out at St Andrew's soup kitchen during the miners' strike of 1893.

Wigan miners out of work gather in the town centre during the 1926 General Strike.

In this double length queue of hungry people, each waits patiently for a welcome loaf of bread during the 1926 General Strike. The bread was given by Jack Langton from outside his Grimshaw's bakery that stood in New Street, Pemberton.

The Kaiser's men – German Prisoners of War were imprisoned at Leigh in a new mill in Atherstone Street which was being built for the Lilford Weaving Co. The PoWs had been captured mainly at Mons, France, in 1915. About 2,000 men were later imprisoned at Leigh. This picture shows the first batch arriving.

Crowds turn out to watch the German PoWs being marched along King Street, Leigh, to their prison camp. In 1915, a 25-year-old German prisoner was shot dead while trying to escape. He was given a military funeral in Leigh Cemetery.

German Prisoners of War playing a game of skittles at their camp in Leigh. In 1918, six died there from influenza during the epidemic which swept Europe, and another six died of natural causes. All were eventually buried in the German war cemetery at Cannock Chase. The Leigh PoW camp closed on 1 June 1919.

Wigan, Leigh and Atherton soldiers of the 5th Battalion, Manchester Regiment marching off to the Front during World War One.

A poignant scene. Hundreds
of local people turned out
on 7 October 1925, to
watch Sir Herbert
A.Lawrence unveil Wigan's
war memorial at the parish
church.

The boys at Whelley Central Elementary School practising air raid precaution drill in 1939. Headmaster at
that time was Mr J.Dean.

This photograph of November 1939, two months after World War Two had been declared, shows a medical team rehearsing for an air raid on Wigan. They are ARP (Air Raid Precaution) wardens. The picture was reproduced in *Picture Post* .

'Register here for the best,' says the notice to customers at this butcher's in Gidow Lane, Wigan, in 1939. Rationing became much more severe in 1940, after the fall of France.

The blizzard of January 1940 caused snow drifts up to 6ft deep around Wigan. This picture, taken on Billinge Road, by Venture Lodge, shows one of them. The war was in its early stages and services ground to a halt. In many places, members of the armed forces were called on to clear roads and railway lines.

Neighbours in Upper Dicconson Street, too, joined in snow clearing during the severe snowfall in the first wartime winter of 1940.

This Armstrong Siddeley of 1934 vintage was one of several local cars pressed into emergency war service in 1940 by local authorities. This one, registered JP1, has black-out mask headlamps and was commandeered by the Auxiliary Fire Service. Note the trailer pump.

ISSUE OF
NEW RATION BOOKS
AND EXAMINATION OF IDENTITY CARDS

YOU NEED 1. Your present Ration Book with the reference leaf filled in.

2. Your Identity Card.

WHERE TO GO

WIGAN

Showroom — Messrs. H. H. Timberlake, Ltd., Library Street, Wigan.   Open daily from 9 a.m. to 5-30 p.m.

UPHOLLAND

The Fuel Overseer's Office, Parliament Street:— Thursday, May 21st and Friday, May 22nd Open from 9-30 a.m. to 8 p.m.

ORRELL

The Council Offices — Tuesday, May 19th and Wednesday, May 20th.   Open from 9-30 a.m. to 8 p.m.

Appley Bridge, Parbold, Shevington Harrock Hill and Wrightington

The Mission Hall, Appley Bridge – Thursday, May 21st and Friday, May 22nd
Parbold Women's Institute – Tuesday, May 19th and Wednesday, May 20th
Shevington Parish Room – Wednesday, May 27th and Thursday, May 28th
The Council School, Mossy Lea, Wrightington – Thursday, May 28th
Offices open from 9-30 a.m. to 8 p.m.

One person may make application for any number, provided all the Main Ration Books and Identity Cards are produced together.

New ration books were issued periodically during World War Two and this was how newspapers informed the public on where and how to obtain them.

Something to celebrate! This is how the neighbours in Langdale Avenue, Queensway, Swinley, celebrated VE Day in May 1945.

St Patrick's School yard Wigan, was the venue for this jolly VE Day party.

All the mums of Lessingham Avenue, Wigan, turned out to make sure the youngsters enjoyed VE Day party time in May 1945.

Happy residents in Ward Street, Hindley, had no barrel to roll out for their celebrations on VE Day 1945, so a metal dolly tub provided the musical accompaniment. The man on the ground was doing a Charlie Chaplin stunt.

Petrol rationing remained in force until long after the war. Extra petrol was allowed for commercial use and contained a red dye and was drawn from special pumps at filling stations. Here, in 1948, county police officers are seen making a roadside check on a motorist's tank. Illegal use of 'Red' petrol led to severe fines.

No wonder these men are smiling! They had just learned that wartime-imposed petrol rationing had ceased. "Petrol coupons? They're no use now," says the garage man. Petrol rationing ended on 27 May 1950 – five years after the war had ended.

Transport and Outings

Horse-drawn fire-engines from all over Lancashire rushed to Wigan's Market Square in 1890 – but there was no fire! The occasion was the 15th annual meeting of Lancashire Fire Brigades Friendly Society to which Wigan was host. Wiganers must have felt safe that day. Hope Congregational Chapel, which had recently been rebuilt, can be seen in the distance.

Here was an early version of meals on wheels! It was the travelling butcher, Bill Christopher in 1891 when he carried on his meat rounds from his house in Millgate.

Atherton Fire Brigade with their first steam fire-engine in the early 1900s. Early brigades were often hampered by the lack of a good water supply.

The Co-op nowadays is a large concern, but when this delivery cart was used in the 1900s by the Wigan & District Equitable Co-operative Society, there were no refrigerated vehicles to transport the beef, pork and mutton around to their customers.

If things got too hot to handle in Hindley in 1890, the locals could call on these lads for help with their horse-drawn Merryweather engine.

In 1900, this dapper couple were the first in Hindley to own a motor car. These cars were the preserve of the wealthy class.

Horse-drawn drays were once a familiar sight around Wigan. This ornate dray belonged to Munro's Wigan branch, who delivered wines and spirits in the area.

Hold on to your hats girls, we're off to breezy Blackpool! Judging by their serious faces some of these Victorian womenfolk from Atherton in 1900 seem a bit apprehensive about the journey.

It was always the tradition in former days for the foreman to wear a bowler hat while the rest of his men would sport cloth caps. This gang of navvies are laying the tram track from Wigan town centre to Poolstock in 1904.

All dressed up and raring to go. Members of Wigan Subscription Bowling Club, off Park Road in 1905, are all set for a summer's day outing aboard the horse-drawn wagonette. Not one man can be seen hatless.

Leigh Fire Brigade in the early days with their gleaming brass helmets.

Not much of importance here you may think. But on this stretch of rail track at Parkside, Golborne, the white marble monument on the left marks the site of a historical tragedy. It commemorates the spot where Britain's first rail fatality occurred. It was during the opening ceremony of the Liverpool-Manchester line in 1829 that former Board of Trade Minister, William Huskisson, MP for Liverpool, stepped out on the line to greet the Duke of Wellington when Stephenson's famous Rocket loco hit and killed him.

Workers constructing railway arches over Queen Street in Leigh in 1863 take a well-earned breather. They were working on the Leigh branch of the Eccles, Tyldesley and Wigan line.

Sightseers gathered to watch men building Henhurst Bridge, Wigan, 90 years ago. The workmen were widening Chapel Lane to allow better traffic flows into and out of the town centre.

A reminder of the great days of steam – and nowhere greater than in Wigan when the town had no fewer than three rail depots as recently as the early 1960s. This giant loco, Royal Naval Division, was used on express services and is pictured at the Spring's Branch Depot. Sadly, the loco was later scrapped. (Picture from *Northern Steam Remembered*, Oxford Publishing Co.)

In the late 1890s the popular form of transport was the tramcar. This double-decker belonging to Wigan Corporation is seen halted by Abbey Lakes Pleasure Grounds on the right.

This formidable bunch of shawled and bonnetted ladies were members of St Andrew's Mothers' Union which met on Thursday afternoons at the turn of the century.

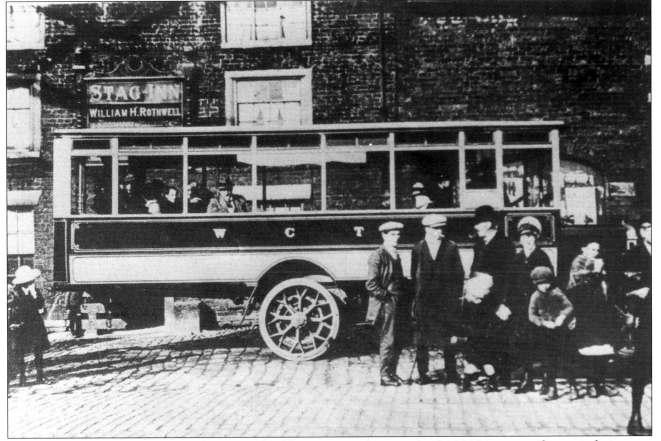

This was Wigan Corporation's first motorised bus. It came into service in 1919 to cover the route between Orrell and Billinge. Here it is outside the Stag Inn at Orrell.

Making roads with granite setts like this at Cross Hillock in Astley around 1920 was a toilsome task. But many of today's old Tarmacadam roads still have these granite sett foundations beneath them.

Are we coming or going? No wonder the flat-capped passenger gives a quizzical glance at the camera. Travelling in this 14-seater taxi around 1920 must have taken some time to fill up with fares. The vehicle was owned by E. & W.Moss of Greenhough Street, Wigan.

No wonder this all-female outing party from the Alison Arms, Wigan, are well wrapped up. Setting out, in 1920 on a wet day, for Southport in a draughty old charabanc like this one was certainly no picnic.

Websters of Wigan used this powerful steam waggon for their furniture removals around 1920. The huge beast had solid metal wheels and had to be stoked up every morning before use.

The fire service in Leigh were proud of their engine of 1922 – including its carbide headlamps, solid tyres and no windscreen. In those days bystanders often stepped in to help and usually proved a hindrance. Of the two firemen on the side, one is ready for action wearing his World War One medals, while the other is in plain clothes.

Today's paramedics wouldn't take too kindly to rushing to an emergency in this early Leigh borough ambulance. Prior to councils taking charge of ambulance services they were run by volunteers of collieries.

Driving a van like this in 1919 in all weathers was no pleasant task. Apart from having no door, the windscreen only covered the lower front window space – and a car heater was then unheard of. Notice the handbrake is on the outside of the vehicle and the headlights are oil-lit.

Solid tyres meant a bumpy ride but it didn't discourage these Hindley folk going on a great outing to Southport in 1922 in a Sheridan coach.

Corless buses were the last independent service to run between Wigan and Chorley. This one is in Spendmore Lane in 1923.

A single-deck electric tram struggles to make the top of the brow as it passes Notre Dame Convent (left) in Standishgate.

Not a smile to be seen on this 1920s outing. Top speed on the chassis says 12mph, so that should not have scared the ladies – or did it? Note the driver's steering wheel was in the middle, with passengers at each side of him. Driver, Fred Ball, worked for Ince Wagon Co.

A Wakes Week at Blackpool prior to World War Two meant that you were comfortably off. Until then it was estimated that two-thirds of the working population went away only for day trips. These Ashton-in-Makerfield residents spent a happy week at Blackpool in 1918. The seaside landladies believed in crowding their guests in and they had a reputation for imposing strict regulations in their apartments.

It seems to have been a hard day's grind for this trio of tired corn mill workers. They were snapped in 1928 outside William Bentley & Sons corn mill in Wigan.

This bone-shaker bicycle was made in 1864 in Wigan by Samuel Meling, seen here in 1929 when his machine was still capable of being used. The family ran Ince Forge for eight generations.

Not much room for any more. Members of St Thomas' Mothers' Union, Caroline Street, Wigan, in 1936 setting sail for Parbold by horse-drawn barge on the Leeds-Liverpool Canal.

This 100-year-old Ben Jonson Bridge, on Warrington Road, Wigan, was one of the first local traffic danger spots to be demolished after World War Two. It was remedied in 1951.

This peaceful, terraced garden in Orrell Mount, Orrell, in 1959 now lies beneath the M6 motorway. It is one of 11 houses compulsory purchased for demolition to make way for the M6 at Orrell. Requests by local councillors to re-route this part to save the houses was refused by the county council on the grounds of cost.

Wigan Central Station, off Millgate, was demolished following the Beeching Report of 1963. At the time the station was closed it was running 26 weekday trains and 11 on Sundays. It was demolished to make a car-park.

Churches, Schools and Bands

The former King Street Baptist Church, Wigan, was formed after a Baptist breakaway from another Wigan Church. The King Street worshippers were later declared sinful for holding a raffle to raise money for church building. The site was bought by the Trustee Savings Bank in 1969.

Villagers still talk about Up Holland's notorious local, George Lyon, a highwayman who was hanged at Lancaster. He was one of the last highway robbers to be hanged there. Strangely, Up Holland villagers brought his body back by cart to give him an honourable burial here in the parish church, despite his infamy.

Homage to a highway man. For over 30 years veteran cyclist Tom Hughes made an annual pilgrimage to Up Holland Church to visit highwayman George Lyon's grave. Lyon was hanged at Lancaster, in 1851. Tom Hughes was a Pemberton miner for 54 years.

Pemberton Colliery Church School at the corner of Foundry Lane was built in 1867 by Colonel Blundell. The school was for boys who worked in that pit, but they had to pay one penny a week for chalk and slates. The building was demolished in 1938.

These were the keen young rugby players of Pemberton Colliery School who chalked up a total of 82 points for and nil points against according to the board seen here in 1909.

These sleepy-eyed boys around 1920 heading the line-up for school were probably half-timers. That is they worked in the mill until 12 noon for one half of the day and attended school in the other. The children are in the Pony Dick Colliery area of Pemberton.

How is this for a double up? This photograph was taken of numerous sets of family brothers who were pupils at the time at Standish Grammar School. It was taken around 1927-28.

It was a big day for the start of Rose Bridge Central School, Ince, when the foundation stone was laid on 17 December 1927, by Councillor George Foster, education committee chairman. What a pity the photographer couldn't raise a smile from somebody.

Walking days were popular events years ago. Here is Pemberton Old Band passing down Cornish Row around 1890 when they were founded. Once, when marching along Wallgate, when playing the triumphal march, an old lady asked them to make less noise. Jokingly they took off their boots and continued playing.

Abram Colliery Prize Brass Band outside Abram Colliery Cricket Club in 1928. This band ceased when the pit became Bickershaw's. It wasn't usual in those days for bandsmen to wear collars and ties with their uniforms.

Dog collar uniforms were preferred by Lower Ince Temperance Band when they played in 1928.

Walking Day was always an occasion to wear one's best. This is Hindley Wesleyan Chapel Sunday School passing along Atherton Road in 1922.

Hindley Walking Day was an occasion when a youngster might get a new suit. This is St Peter's Church contingent in 1937 in Atherton Road.

Whit Monday church processions were always a popular spectacle for Wigan area folk. Here are members of St Joseph's Church, passing along Standishgate by Notre Dame Convent in the 1920s.

All Saints' School, Appleby Bridge, keep smartly in line during a 1920s Walking Day procession.

Whit Monday processions were enjoyed by all the family who saw it as a great day out. In this section of St Joseph's processionists are Bishop Dobson, the Revd Parkinson, the Revd Van Wassentove and the Mayor of Wigan, James Carey.

It was a day of sunshine when the foundation stone of the church of St John the Divine, Coppull, was laid in June 1911. The bottle on the platform was laid beneath the stone and it contained a scroll, coins of the day and copies of *The Times* and *Chorley Guardian*.

Dense crowds line the pavement to see St Patrick's taking part in the Wigan Whit Walks of 1926.

Crowds used to pack the routes to watch the Whitsuntide religious processions go by. This one is passing the old Convent School, Standishgate in 1935.

A peaceful scene of the Angel Hotel (left) and St Thomas' Church, Ashton-in-Makerfield. But not so in 1870 when a large section of the congregation jeered and threatened their new vicar, the Revd Page-Oldham, because he wore a surplice instead of the usual black gown. The mob yelled, "No popery," each time he appeared in the pulpit in a surplice. The row ceased when the vicar resumed a black gown and he was forgiven, but sadly the vicar died from a heart attack a few months afterwards.

Wigan Parish Church has a colourful history. The present church is the third built on the site since its recording in the 1086 Domesday Book. In 1643 the parish church was besieged by Cromwell's troops attacking Royalists inside. In 1850, the new church was consecrated. The tower goes back to medieval times.

St Aidan's, Billinge, was rebuilt in 1718 after falling into disrepair. Up to the Reformation it had been a Catholic Church and during Queen Mary's reign villagers, led by fanatical James Winstanley, entered the church and wrecked it along with many vestments.

St Patrick's parishioners carry a statue of their patron saint in the Whit Monday procession in 1966. This also happened to be the last procession of its kind and so ended a long and colourful tradition.

Sports and Personalities

Along with near rivals Leigh, and other North-West rugby clubs, Wigan broke away from the Great Northern Union in 1895 to form the Rugby League. Jim Yates was one of the formidable Wigan side soon afterwards. They played on land near Dicconson Street before Central Park was founded in 1909.

This proud squad brought glory to a small town in 1905-06. Leigh RL shook the sporting world by winning the Championship trophy for the first time in their history. However, it was a long wait for the next Championship trophy – 1982 under Alex Murphy.

And this is the Leigh RL team that again took that Championship trophy in 1982. The Hilton Park outfit snatched the prize from under the noses of the major clubs.

The all-conquering Wigan RL team of 1908-09 who won the Lancashire Cup, the Northern Rugby League trophy and the West Lancashire League.

Included in this Wigan RL team of the 1914 era is the much-famed player Jim Sullivan. Front row (left to right) are George Hesketh, Sid Jerram, John Ring, Gerry Shay, Jim Sullivan, Sid Boyde and Don Hurcombe. Among those on the back row are Percy Caldrick, Will Hodder, George Banks and John Sherrington.

The Cherry and Whites – 1920 style. Wigan RL captain at that time Sid Jerram is in the centre holding the ball. The bucket, on the right, is where the trainer kept his 'magic' sponge.

A memento of 1921 when Leigh RL met Australia at Leigh's Mather Lane ground. Leigh lost 17-4. Their skipper (left) was Mooney. Next to him was Leigh's Mayor, Councillor Holden, complete with his fashionable spats.

The Wigan side of 1947-48 contained these all-time greats. Back row (left to right): Ryan, Gee, Blan, Ward, Hilton, Bowen. Front row: Banks, Lawrenson, Barton, Bradshaw, Egan (captain), Mountford and Ratcliffe.

Wigan RL skipper Joe Egan was chaired around Maine Road after leading his side to a 13-2 victory over Dewsbury in the 1947 RL Championship.

All aboard for Wembley. Wigan RL fans, all smartly dressed, on 1 May 1948, at Wallgate Station. The occasion was the Cup Final between Wigan and Bradford Northern when the cherry and white lads romped to victory.

A Central Park crowd of 42,500 in 1949 was then a record attendance for the Wigan ground when the club met Warrington. The record leapt to 47,747 in 1969 when Wigan clashed with rivals St Helens. Since then new ground safety rules have been imposed.

The name of Wigan is synonymous with its Rugby League club. Here Cec Mountford is seen at Maine Road after Wigan beat Huddersfield 20-2 in the 1950 Championship Final before a crowd of 65,500.

Wigan RL reigned supreme in 1952. This is the victorious team which defeated Bradford Northern 13-6 in the Championship Final held at Huddersfield.

A rapturous welcome awaited the Wigan RL Cup team in 1958 after their hard-fought 13-9 victory over Workington Town. Wigan were then bringing the Cup home for the fifth time and the first since 1951.

Glory Days! The 1959 Wigan team romped to a 30-13 victory over Hull only a year after many of the players had recorded a 13-9 Wembley success over Workington. Back row (left to right): McGurrin, Brotherton, Boston, McTigue, Sayer, Cherrington, Barton, Collier. Front row: Thomas, Sullivan, Ashton, Bolton, Evans, Cunliffe. Inset: Griffiths, Holden.

Anyone remember this Wigan RL team of 1965-66? Back row (left to right) they are: L.Gilfedder, D.Gardiner, H.Major, T.Woosey, B.McTigue, W.Boston, G.Lyon. Middle row: D.Stephens, C.Hesketh, T.Lake, E.Ashton (captain), R.Ashby, C.Clarke, A.Stephens. Front row: C.Hill, F.Parr.

Labour Party leader Neil Kinnock joins the Mayor and Mayoress of Wigan, Councillor Peter Hall, and his wife Margaret, in the home-coming celebration of Wigan RL winning the Championship in 1985 when they beat Hull.

Wigan Borough FC's 1923-24 team. Because of Rugby League's attraction, it took several attempts for soccer to get a footing in Wigan. Before Wigan Athletic was formed, four other soccer clubs representing the town had failed. Wigan Town, Wigan County and Wigan United were short-lived. They were followed by Wigan Borough, who joined the Football League's Third Division North in 1920. They attracted a record crowd at Springfield Park when 33,000 saw them lose to Sheffield Wednesday in the FA Cup. Wigan Borough resigned from the League in 1931 and were re-formed in 1932 as Wigan Athletic in the Lancashire Combination.

Wigan Athletic's 1933-34 team and officials. This side won the Cheshire League championship, having been turned down by the Football League's Third Division North. In those days Latics played in cherry and white halves.

Wigan Athletic's 1949-50 team. Back row (left to right): E.Berry (trainer), Tolley, Whiteside, Cunliffe, Sharratt, Parkinson, Shirley, Bob Pryde (manager). Front row: Finan, Rothwell, Lomax, Taylor, Pollard. The Latics finally made it into the Football League in 1978.

Wigan was a hotbed for rugged wrestlers, especially in the 1920s. These determined grapplers and their seconds are at Springfield Park football ground before a match. The bouts sometimes lasted for up to 50 rounds and attracted big crowds. Local champion at that time was Bob Silcock.

Three sporting greats – pint-sized flyweight world champion boxer Peter Kane shakes hands with RL player Arthur Atkinson of Castleford. Peter Kane of Golborne held the title from 1938 to 1943. He died in 1991. On the right of the picture is Wigan RL super goalscorer Jim Sullivan at a Central Park reception in the 1930s.

Remember 'Romeo' Joe Critchley? He was the popular 1960s wrestler. The cloaked 'grunt-and-groaner' is seen holding a Wigan toddler from the audience at Butlin's Holiday Camp in Pwllheli while the boy's parents look on. Wakes Weeks were a popular time for holidays in North Wales and Blackpool for Lancashire folk.

The Premier Wheeler's of Lower Ince pictured in 1928 in front of Bushell's farmhouse.

Even avant-garde women golfers wouldn't want to be seen not wearing a hat for a round of golf. This picture was taken in 1922, soon after Dean Wood Golf Club, Up Holland, was opened.

What? Women wearing plus-fours! This game in 1929, at Dean Wood Golf Club, Up Holland, shows these sporty-type women golfers were not going to be outdone by any male chauvinists.

George Formby (senior), was born at Ashton-under-Lyne. He had a wretched childhood but his undaunted spirit raised him from singing and dancing for coppers in the streets to the music-halls of Lancashire as a top entertainer. Formby has signed the card 'Daft and knows it'.

During their 20 years residence in Wigan, George Formby (senior) and his family lived in several different homes including Dicconson Street, Hindley House and Malvern House (later called Linacre House) which is pictured here in Wigan Lane.

Turned out nice again! George Formby and his wife Beryl, a former stage dancer, setting off in 1951 on one of his world show business tours.

Scottish-American tycoon Andrew Carnegie received the Freedom of Wigan when he visited in 1909. Five years earlier he had donated a large sum of money to build Pemberton Library. Here he is seen with the Mayor of Wigan, Alderman S.Woods.

In 1936, George Formby (junior) presents a rug embroidered with the old Wigan motto, to the Mayor of Wigan, Councillor Peter Winstanley. Beryl Formby, George's wife, is on the extreme left.

From joy to sadness. George Formby and his fiancée, Pat Howson, a 36-year-old Preston schoolteacher, celebrate their engagement a few weeks after George's wife, Beryl, died. However, six weeks before the wedding date, George, aged 56, died in Mount Street Hospital, Preston, on 6 March 1961, from a heart attack. Pat, whom George had known since her childhood, died a few years later.

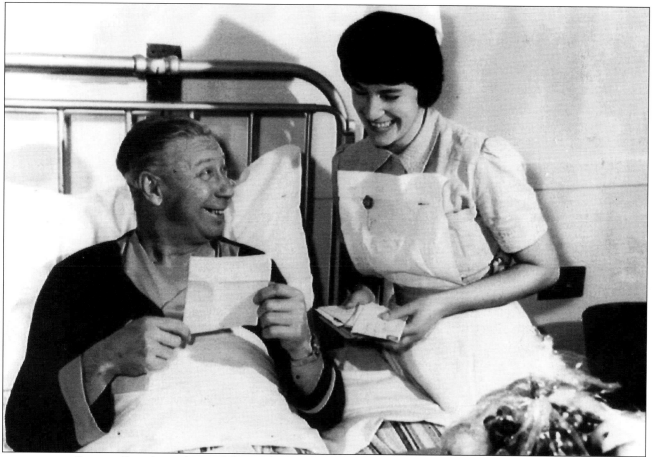

George Formby enjoys a joke with a nurse in hospital shortly before he died in 1961.

Right: The miners' champion Joe Gormley was born in Ashton-in-Makerfield. As president of the National Union of Mineworkers he challenged the Tory Government over a union wage claim in 1974 and the Government, under Ted Heath, lost the battle. The picture shows Joe as an NUM delegate. *Far right:* The Miners' Peer. After retiring as NUM president in 1982, Joe Gormley was granted a peerage and returned to live in the Wigan area. He lived in a bungalow at Shevington and died aged 75. Here Lord Gormley is seen holding a bust of himself carved in coal.

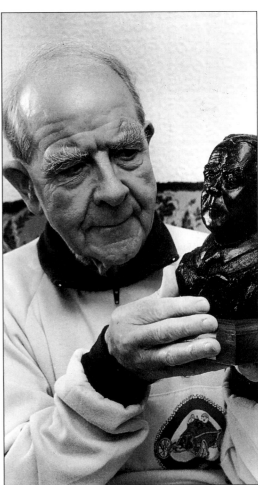

Wigan-born 'top cop' Sir James Anderton (right) visited his home town after receiving his knighthood in 1991. The head of Greater Manchester Police retired that year and here he receives a Wigan welcome of a Wigan RL teddy bear, a jar of Uncle Joe's Mint Balls, an outsize pair of clogs and two Poole's pies. The presenter is Wigan's Chief Superintendent, Gordon Burton.

Royal Visits

A momentous occasion for the Wigan area occurred in 1898 when the Prince of Wales (later Edward VII) stayed at Garswood Hall, the home of his friend Lord Gerard and his family. Lord Gerard is fourth from the left beside the Prince. Lady Randolph Churchill, mother of Sir Winston, sits holding the pet dog.

Wallgate decked out in patriotic style to mark the Coronation of King Edward VII in 1902. The Coronation was postponed from the original date of 20 June to 9 August because the King had to undergo an emergency operation for appendicitis. However, Wigan had already planned its three-day celebrations for the Coronation and the town went ahead with them in June.

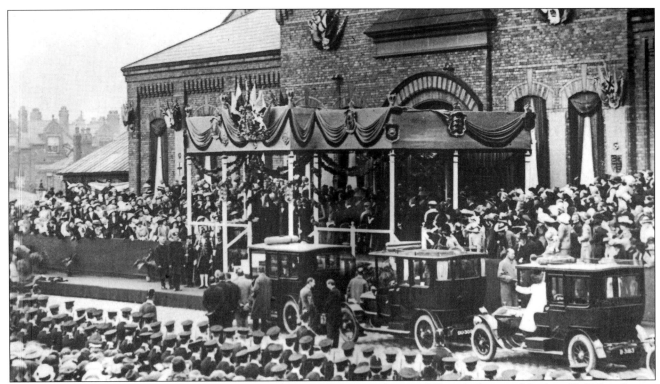

The motorcade bearing King George V and Queen Mary arrives at Wigan's former Market Hall for the Royal visit in 1913.

King George V and Queen Mary being greeted by civic dignitaries when they visited Wigan on 10 July 1913. The Royal couple arrived via Darlington Street at a specially erected Market Hall stage. A procession of schoolchildren to the Market Hall was led by Pemberton Total Abstinence Band.

King George V and Queen Mary's Silver Jubilee in 1935 was celebrated in style by the neighbours in Margaret Street, Whelley. The children received a souvenir mug to mark the occasion.

The King who was never crowned. The Prince of Wales (later Edward VIII and the Duke of Windsor) pictured on his visit to Wigan in the late 1920s. It was around this time that he visited the depression-hit areas of the South Wales coalfields and made his never forgotten remark, "Something must be done," after he saw the poverty there.

Royalty made several visits to the Wigan area in the space of a very few years. In March 1986, Queen Elizabeth II opened the Wigan Pier complex. Here Prince Philip is seen following the Queen aboard the water bus during their historic visit.

It isn't often a man greets a monarch in his braces! Queen Elizabeth II waves to the cheering crowds as she steps off the barge at Wigan Pier's Heritage Museum, which she officially opened in March 1986. The man wearing braces was an attendant, appropriately dressed for such an occasion.

The Queen and Prince Philip bid farewell at Wigan Station at the end of their 1986 Royal visit.

A conveyor belt of man-size tissues coming off the assembly line caught the eye of Princess Anne at Ashton-in-Makerfield in March 1986, when she opened a new paper products factory which also manufactured toilet rolls.

The Prince and
Princess of Wales
were apparently
still a happily
married couple in
April 1986, when
this photograph
was taken as they
toured an Ashton-
in-Makerfield
bakery firm's
exhibition. They
smile as they sign
the visitors' book.

A visit by helicopter to Wigan by Princess Anne, in December 1989, included a visit to Wymott Prison
where she unveiled a commemorative plaque. Here she is applauded by the prison governor.

Little Kathy Barnes, of Up Holland, greets Princess Diana and Prince Charles with a posy and she receives a Royal smile from each in return during their visit to Ashton-in-Makerfield in 1986.

Princess Anne was given a protective overall when she toured Heinz's Kitt Green factory on 1 December 1989, to open the work's new extension. Here she turns to look at a mountain of canned beans.

Tragedy struck soon after this photograph was taken at the Heinz food factory, Kitt Green, Wigan, on 1 December 1989. Minutes after Mr Derek Dollman (left), a factory manager, had presented this giant cheque to Princess Anne for her Save the Children Fund, he collapsed. He died two hours later in Wigan Infirmary. By then the Princess had left the factory and was informed of the tragedy afterwards and was saddened to hear of it.

A tired Princess Anne leaves after her 1989 visit to Wigan, accompanied by Colonel John Timms, Lord Lieutenant of Greater Manchester.

The Princess Royal, Princess Anne, made her third visit to Wigan in 12 months when she opened Ingersoll Rand's new wing at Hindley Green in September, 1990.

Her Royal Highness, the Duchess of Gloucester, visited Whelley Hospital in September 1990, to open the Elderly Care Unit. While there she was introduced to this smart line of nurses.

What is it that Princess Anne finds so attractive about Wigan? Here she is making her fourth visit to the borough in a year, in November 1990. This time it was to open Wigan Hospice, in Poolstock Lane, where she is seen chatting with some of the officials.

Subscribers

Dorothy Jean Blythe

Frank & Maureen Brindle

A B Cabinets

Mrs Emily E Clark

Debbie J.Daniels & Joe S Pledger

Dianne Davies

Keith W Fanning

William Farrimond

John Grainger

Susan Catherine Grainger

Julia Ellen Gray

Lucy Catherine Green

Graham Anthony Hales

Frances Patricia Hill

David Eric Holland

Lee Kerry Jade Holland

Peter Johnson

Kenneth & Elsie Lucas

Tony Robert Mason

Charles & Phyllis Melling

James Needle

David Plumpton

Leonard Prescott

Anton Charles Rippon

Patricia Ann Rippon

Nicola Jane Rippon

Philip John Southall

Dennis Squires

Ian Watkinson

John Winstanley